the Weekend Crafter®

Beading

the
Weekend
Crafter®

Beading

From Necklaces to Napkin Rings
20 Easy & Creative Projects
to Make in a Weekend

PAIGE GILCHRIST BLOMGREN

LARK
BOOKS

A Division of Sterling
Publishing Co., Inc.
New York

ART DIRECTOR & PRODUCTION:
CHRIS BRYANT

PHOTOGRAPHY:
EVAN BRACKEN

ILLUSTRATIONS:
ORRIN LUNDGREN

EDITORIAL ASSISTANCE:
HEATHER SMITH

PRODUCTION ASSISTANCE:
HANNES CHAREN

Library of Congress Cataloging-in-Publication Data
Blomgren, Paige Gilchrist.
    Beading : from necklaces to napkin rings, 20 easy & creative projects
to make in a weekend / Paige Gilchrist Blomgren.
        p. cm. — (The weekend crafter)
    Includes index.
    ISBN 1-57990-091-7
    1. Beadwork. I. Title. II. Series.
TT860.B59   1999
745.58'2—dc21   98-45007
                                                                  CIP

20 19 18 17 16 15 14 13 12 11

Published by Lark Books, a division of
Sterling Publishing Co., Inc.
387 Park Avenue South, New York, N.Y. 10016

© 1998, Lark Books

Distributed in Canada by Sterling Publishing,
c/o Canadian Manda Group, 165 Dufferin Street
Toronto, Ontario, Canada M6K 3H6

Distributed in the United Kingdom by GMC Distribution Services,
Castle Place, 166 High Street, Lewes, East Sussex, England BN7 1XU

Distributed in Australia by Capricorn Link (Australia) Pty Ltd.,
P.O. Box 704, Windsor, NSW 2756 Australia

If you have questions or comments about this book, please contact:
Lark Books
67 Broadway
Asheville, NC 28801
(828) 253-0467

Manufactured in China

ISBN 13: 978-1-57990-091-5
ISBN 10: 1-57990-091-7

For information about custom editions, special sales, premium and corporate
purchases, please contact Sterling Special Sales Department at 800-805-5489 or
specialsales@sterlingpub.com.

CONTENTS

Introduction:

So Many Beads, So Little Time 6

Bead Basics 8

Design Basics 18

Jewelry & Accessory Projects

    Strung Necklace 24

    Knotted Cord Necklace 26

    Amulet Pouch 28

    Memory Wire Bracelet 32

    Stretch Bracelet 34

    Drop Earrings 36

    Wire Hoop Earrings 38

    Handmade Pin 40

    Zipper Pull 42

    Hair Sticks 44

    Rainbow Baseball Cap 46

Jewelry & Accessories Gallery 48

Beaded Object Projects

    Napkin Rings 52

    Bath Bottle 54

    Painted Box 56

    Beaded Greeting Card 58

    Charmed Beaded Basket 60

    Fan Pull 62

    Picture Frame 64

    Bead-wrapped Bottle 66

    Fringed Bookmark 68

Beaded Objects Gallery 70

Contributing Designers 77

Acknowledgments 79

Index 79

A Note About Suppliers 80

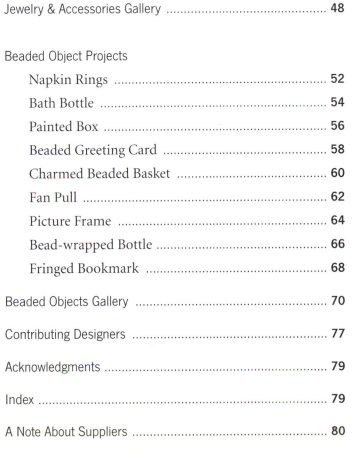

INTRODUCTION

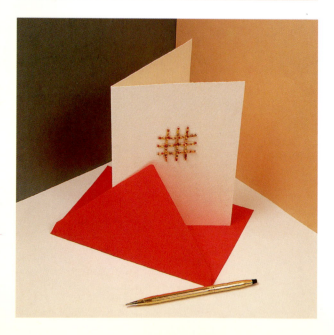

BEFORE YOU START, forget beads for a moment. Focus first on that enticing little word in this book's title, the one that both attracts you and makes you nervous: *weekend*. As in *Weekend* Crafter. Let's just consider the concept of *weekend*.

When you close your eyes and travel in your imagination to that place you know as weekend, do you relax your shoulder and neck muscles as you envision 48 glorious hours of self-indulgence spreading out before you? Uninterrupted time? Quite, peaceful, demand-free time? *Your* time? Of course you don't.

Your eyes immediately pop back open and begin frantically searching for a scrap of paper and a pen. Your tension points stiffen as you start feverishly listing things you just remembered you forgot: birthday gift for the party on Saturday, food for the visitors passing through on Sunday, trip to the vet. Not to mention the list you'd like to forget but couldn't if you tried: the yard, the garage, the laundry, the stack of work you carried home Friday night.

You'll be relieved to know that the designers who contributed projects to this book understand real-life weekends. Their beaded jewelry, bottles, baskets, boxes, and more are designed to allow you to plunge in and create something beautiful out of beads in a real weekend, even if you have to do it in intervals.

FOR EXAMPLE:

Driving the team carpool on Saturday morning?

Between drop-off and pick-up, purchase the supplies for the project you've chosen to work on. For a number of projects in this book, especially the jewelry projects, one stop at a well-stocked bead store will do it for both materials and tools. For other projects, you'll also need to purchase (or recycle) an object to bead upon—a cap, a picture frame, or a bottle of bath salts, for instance. Finally, a few projects call for a trip to a fabric store for ribbon, a craft store for paints and brushes, or a hardware store for a standard item or two.

Got an hour on Saturday afternoon after the grocery store or the gym?

Set up a work space, spread out your supplies, and start easing into your project. If you've never held a pair of round-nose pliers in your hand before (let alone used them to create a wire spiral to serve as a stopper for a string of beads), use the illustrated instructions in the Bead Basics section as a guide and experiment with a few twists and turns. Now would also be a good time to apply the base coat of paint for the painted box project, create your design grid for the beaded greeting card project, or handle any other simple prep work.

Is everyone else in the house crowded around the VCR on Saturday night?

Join them! Especially if you've chosen a project that involves a lot of bead stringing (such as the charmed beaded basket) or wire twisting (such as the picture frame), this is the perfect time to clear off a spot between the pizza and the popcorn and make some headway.

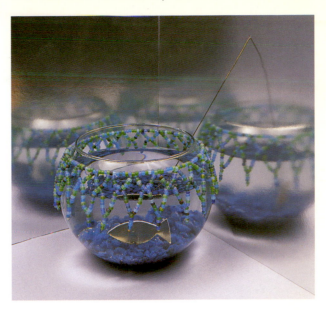

Have you hit that part of Sunday when you finally have something in the oven and the last load on spin cycle?

Celebrate by diving into your project. This is your chance to play with patterns, experiment with technique, and perfect your design.

You're winding down. Are book bags packed, briefcases reloaded, floors sparkling (or at least swept) and laundry folded (clean piles in baskets will do)?

Time for gratification: wrapping the last strands of beaded wire to form a set of napkin rings, sewing the final piece of fringe on your bookmark, or tying the knots and attaching the clasp on a new necklace to wear tomorrow morning.

You see, the fact that Monday morning will actually arrive is something we've been keeping in mind all along. Complete artistic fulfillment may be a bit much to ask of a single book on weekend beading, but the 20 beginner-friendly projects contained here, each with simple instructions and how-to photos, *are* designed to provide you with a sense of accomplishment.

There's support too. The Bead Basics section starts with an overview of beads themselves and proceeds right on through supplies, tools, and common techniques. The accompanying photos are like a trip through the aisles of a bead store, so you know exactly what to look for when you're in one yourself. The Design Basics section covers everything from classic color combinations to standard stringing patterns, so you can make creative choices with confidence. And gallery photos provide inspiration for what you might tackle next.

So, you don't see a free weekend on your calendar anytime soon? Didn't think so. This is just the book for you.

BEAD BASICS

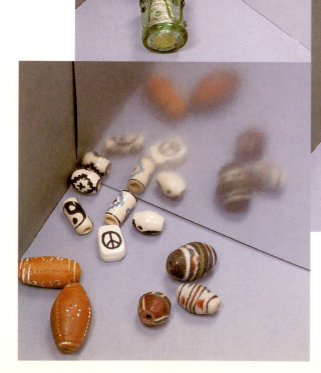

TOP LEFT: Handmade glass beads

TOP RIGHT: India glass beads

CENTER LEFT: Venetian glass barrel beads

CENTER RIGHT: Beads of horn, bone, and wood

BOTTOM LEFT, CLOCKWISE FROM TOP: Peruvian ceramic beads, sand-cast beads from Africa, clay barrel beads

BOTTOM RIGHT: Beads of semiprecious stone

Beads

If it's got a hole you can put a string through, it's a bead. Happily, the definition expands almost endlessly from there. From iridescent cubes and bright glass tubes to chunks of semiprecious stone and exotic silver cones, beads come in enough shapes, sizes, colors, and materials (see Figure 1) to suit any artistic style.

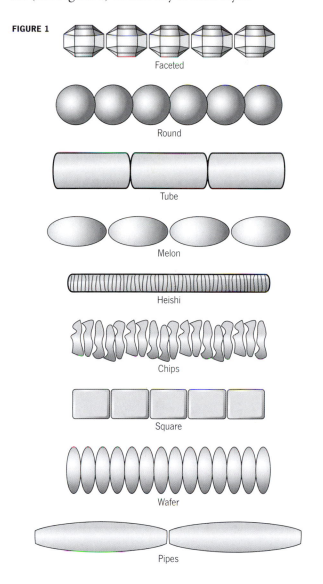

FIGURE 1

Faceted

Round

Tube

Melon

Heishi

Chips

Square

Wafer

Pipes

SIZES

Beads are measured in millimeters, with the size referring to the diameter of the bead, so you know how much space one will take up when it's strung. (Drop beads, with holes through the top, are the exception. Their measurement typically refers to the length of the bead.) The circles in Figure 2 are shown in actual size. Figure 3 provides a comparison of millimeters to inches.

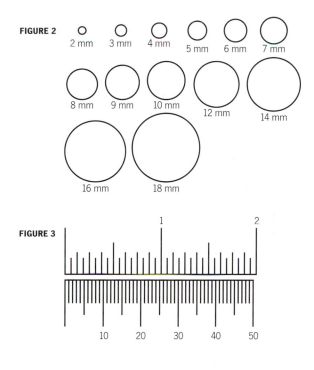

FIGURE 2 2 mm 3 mm 4 mm 5 mm 6 mm 7 mm 8 mm 9 mm 10 mm 12 mm 14 mm 16 mm 18 mm

FIGURE 3

Seed Beads

Seed beads (yes, they get their name from the tiny kernels they resemble) follow a different measuring system. These small glass beads are sized according to number; the higher the number, the smaller the bead. Size 6 seed beads are the most widely available; they're also the seed beads most frequently used for projects in this book. Don't be unnerved if you see them referred to in catalogs or bead shops as 6°, 6/0, or "E" beads—they're all the same thing. Delicas are another common type of seed bead with a special name. They're about the same as a size 12 seed bead, almost cube shaped, and feature large holes that make them easy to string.

Like other beads, seed beads vary in color (topaz to kelly green), shape (triangular to faceted), and finish (matte to metallic).

LEFT TO RIGHT: Delicas, bugle beads, size 10 seed beads, size 11 seed beads, 4x4 cubes

Bead thread

Bugle Beads

Technically a kind of seed bead, these long, cylindrical beads range from 2 mm to 30 mm in length, vary in width, and come in most of the fabulous finishes and colors of other seed beads.

Beading Materials and Tools

In a nutshell, the projects in this book are about stringing (or wiring) beads together and attaching them to other objects. Familiarity with a few materials and some basic tools and techniques is all you need to get started.

THREAD, CORD, AND WIRE

Bead Thread

Silk and nylon bead thread are sold on individual cards and on bulk spools in a variety of colors and thicknesses. Choose thread that is thin enough to go easily through the smallest hole you are stringing (several times, if necessary), yet strong enough to support the weight of the beads. If your thread frays as you force it through, chances are the finished project will have a limited life span. Nylon thread tends to be slightly stronger and more resistant to fraying; silk stretches less over time and knots better.

To make sure the thread is not a noticeable part of your project, match the thread color to the beads. Otherwise, choose a color that is lighter than the beads.

Tigertail and Other Flexible Beading Wires

The advantages of tigertail, a tiny steel cable coated with nylon, are that it's strong, flexible, and durable. Plus, it's stiff enough to use without a needle and, though it doesn't knot well because of the stiffness, you can finish the ends easily with crimp beads. On the downside, it tends to kink, and it drapes well only with larger, heavier beads. Many beaders love the new flexible synthetic beading wire now on the market. This super-strong stringing material is sold under a variety of brand names, comes in various colors and thicknesses, and, when using the smallest diameter, is easier to knot.

Flexible beading wire

Assortment of decorative cords

Spools of 24-gauge wire, 8-gauge copper wire, memory wire

Decorative Cords

Decorative cords aren't meant to be hidden like beading wire and thread. They're often a featured part of the finished product.

LEATHER CORD lends itself to funky, chunky ethnic beads and more casual looks, and it holds knots with style.

WAXED LINEN and waxed or unwaxed cotton cord come in all the colors of the rainbow. Simply tie knots at the ends to finish them off, or use a variety of clasps and endings.

RATTAIL, much prettier than the name implies, is a supple cord with a satin finish. You can find it in a range of shades, twisted or smooth.

ELASTIC CORD comes in multiple colors and even metallic finishes, providing good stringing material for everything from anklets to ponytail holders.

HEMP is gaining popularity as a beading cord; it adds a textured, fibrous look to pieces featuring heavier beads.

Wire

A number of the projects in this book use wire of one form or another to twist, wrap, and attach beads to objects. Occasionally, the wire is meant to be behind the scenes, but most often, it's a shiny, showy part of the final design.

Wire is available in bead stores and craft shops, and comes in a myriad of metals and thicknesses. In this book, we'll be using copper and sterling silver. Gold-filled wire is common too. Typically, wire is sold in spools, and it's identified by gauge. The higher the gauge, the thinner the wire. So, the 34-gauge wire used to wrap beads around the wire basket on page 60 is as thin as some thread, while the 16-gauge wire used for the hair sticks on page 44 is hefty.

Memory wire is popular for bracelet making. As the name suggests, it springs back into its coiled shape after being strung with beads. You can purchase it in packages of usually 20 to 40 coils and snip off as much as you need to work with. (To save wear and tear on your wire cutters, simply bend this sturdy wire back and forth with a pair of pliers to break off the piece you need.)

NEEDLES

With beading wires, you can string without a needle. Heavy synthetic cords offer the same advantage—just dip the end in instant glue to stiffen it, and go. But for many projects, you'll need a needle.

When you're not working with tiny beads or intricate patterns, twisted-wire needles, which are big-eyed and bendable, will make you happiest. Threading the large eye is painless. It closes up when forced through the first bead, but can be easily reopened with an awl or a pin when you need to rethread.

For stringing beads with small holes or for weaving in and out of tight spaces, use beading needles that resemble standard sewing "sharps." They're numbered according to size (10, 13, and 15, for example) and, as with wire,

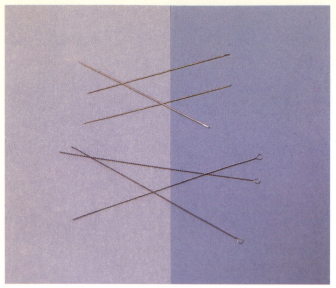

Standard beading needles (top) and big-eyed, twisted-wire needles

FINDINGS

Findings are the manufactured metal pieces (from ear wires to necklace clasps) used in making jewelry and other items. Wide assortments of these attachments and fasteners are available in bead shops and craft stores everywhere—simply knowing they exist in ready-to-use form is a relief. The projects in this book make use of some of the most basic findings.

Clasps

Clasps make it possible to open and close the ends of necklaces and bracelets. They come in styles and metals to match every design, with loops at the end that need to be attached to your beading string. You have several hardware options for connecting string to clasp.

the larger the number, the thinner the needle. Be easy on yourself and choose the largest needle that will go through your bead. Needle and seed bead numbers match, but you should choose a needle that is one size smaller (one number larger) than your seed beads if it is necessary to pass through them more than once.

If the single act of threading tiny-eyed beading needles seems more of a feat than stringing the necklace and making an outfit to go with it, cut the thread at an angle, coat it with beeswax, and squeeze it flat before trying again.

GLUE

Glue is critical if you want to keep your projects from unraveling. Most common is fast-drying bead glue or bead cement, sold in craft stores in small tubes. Don't knot anything off without adding a dab of this glue to seal it. But here's a caveat: though it comes with a pointed applicator, if you use it, you risk adding glue not only to the knot but to nearby beads. Apply the glue first to a needle, straight pin, or toothpick, then dab it on your knot. In a pinch, clear nail polish works well for securing knots, but avoid craft or gel adhesives. They coat the surface without saturating the knot and holding it tight.

Industrial strength adhesive and sealant, available in large tubes in most bead stores, does the job for nearly every other kind of sticking project, whether you're affixing beads to picture frames or gluing beaded wire to wood.

CLOCKWISE FROM BOTTOM LEFT: Eyeglass holder clasps, an assortment of necklace clasps, crimp beads

CLOCKWISE FROM BOTTOM LEFT: Bead tips, split rings, jump rings

BEAD TIPS are one of the most common connectors for necklaces (they're used on the strung necklace project on page 24). They hold and hide the final knot, then attach to a clasp.

Thread your needle through a bead tip (with the tip's hook facing outward, toward the end of the necklace or bracelet). Knot the thread, tuck it into the cup of the bead tip, and knot again. Dot your knots with bead cement and clip the thread tail close to the knots. Attach the bead tip's hook to the end of your clasp and close the hook with chain-nose pliers (see Figure 4).

FIGURE 4

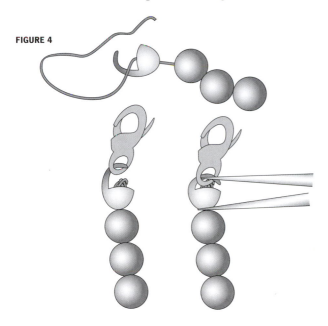

Clamshell bead tips are also available. They close up (as the name suggests) and hide your knots completely. Follow the same process you would use for a regular bead tip, but use chain-nose pliers to close the clamshell once your knots have been dotted with glue (see Figure 5).

FIGURE 5

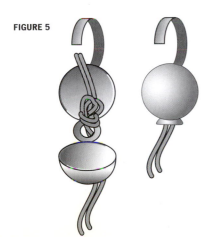

You can attach one bead tip, string your piece of jewelry, then add the second bead tip. Or, if you're still experimenting with your design, you can string all your beads and add both bead tips when you're finished.

CRIMP BEADS are another way to connect a necklace or bracelet strand to a clasp. Most often used with tigertail and flexible beading wires (which knot poorly unless you're using the smallest diameter), crimp beads are small metal sleeves that hold tightly onto what's inside once they're pinched or "crimped."

Simply string a crimp bead onto the end of your string, add your clasp, then go back through the crimp bead to form a loop around the clasp. Thread the end of your string back through a few beads, then slide the crimp bead tight against the clasp and flatten it with chain-nose pliers (see Figure 6). Repeat with the other end of the clasp and the other end of your string.

FIGURE 6

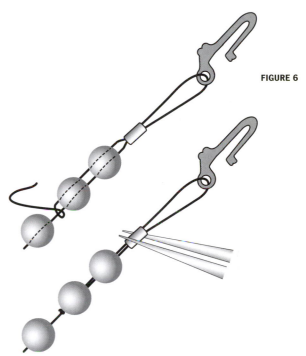

Jump Rings

Jump rings are wire circles that are split somewhere on their circumference—just the thing for connecting a charm to a piece of jewelry (see Figure 7) or a loop to a clasp . A jump ring connects the ending wire loop to a clasp on the zipper pull on page 42. For the bracelet projects on pages 32 and 35, you also have the option of using jump rings to connect your charms to the stringing material.

FIGURE 7

Don't pry the jump ring open by spreading the ends farther apart and enlarging the circle; this weakens the ring. Instead, use two pairs of pliers to twist the ring open, moving the ends in opposite directions (see Figure 8). Add your charm, connect the ring to the bracelet or necklace, and close the ring by reversing the motion you used to open it.

FIGURE 8

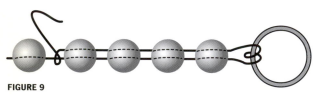

FIGURE 9

You could also finish a string of beads with a jump ring by taking the needle through the ring, wrapping the thread twice, then threading back through several beads and knotting the thread (see Figure 9). Needle back through several more beads, knot again, dot both knots with bead cement, and clip the thread tails. The jump ring can then be attached to a clasp.

Split rings are a variation of the standard jump ring. They're made up of double circles of wire and resemble a tiny key ring.

Bead Caps and Spacers

Bead caps are decorative features that top off the end of a bead and hide the hole. Spacers are tiny, disk-shaped fillers that separate beads and add accents.

Various bead caps and spacers

Head Pins and Eye Pins

These straight pieces of wire come in various lengths and are sold by the dozen. Head pins are used in this book's bath bottle project (page 54) to create dangles of beads. The flat head at one end of the pin (like a small nail head) keeps the beads from falling. Eye pins are another variation, with an eye "stopper" at the end instead of a head. With either type, add beads to the pin, then loop the end opposite the stopper around whatever you want to attach it to.

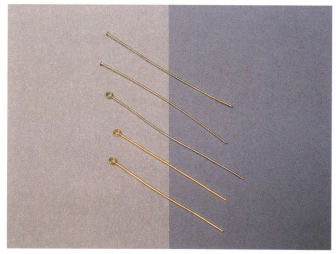

Head pins (top) and eye pins

Earring Findings

Purchased ear wires and handmade hoops are featured in projects in this book. You'll find ear wires in the form of French, Spanish, and kidney wires. Though slightly different in how they stay in the pierced lobe, all function in basically the same way. One end goes in your ear, the other has a loop for attaching beaded creations. When starting out, make sure you select wires that have loops that can be opened and closed. That way, you can simply add your finished beadwork to the loop. If the loop on the finding doesn't open, you'll have to incorporate it into the beading—not a huge problem, but nice to avoid for your first few projects.

Many posts also come with loops at the bottom for attaching dangles of beads, as do certain designs of clip- and screw-on findings.

Other Findings

Beyond the basics, bead stores, craft shops, and catalogs stock gadgets that can form the foundation for endless beaded projects. As you use the projects in this book as springboards for your own designs, you can experiment with everything from purchased pin and barrette backs to bolo tie hardware and key rings.

TOOLS

Pliers and Cutters

Though the options on the tool rack are many, you can make the projects in this book (and countless others) with just a few basics.

ROUND-NOSE PLIERS are important for making loops. It's best not to choose pliers with a serrated jaw when you're working with wire; they'll mar the metal.

CHAIN-NOSE PLIERS (rounded on the outside surfaces but flat on the inside) are good for gripping wire.

WIRE CUTTERS allow you to trim and snip; they should cut flush. Diagonal cutters are excellent for getting into small spaces to nip off ends that can snag clothing and skin.

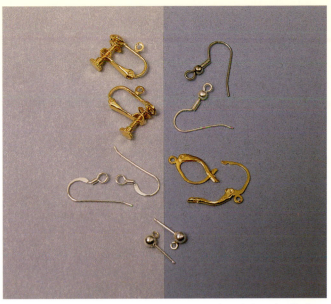

Assorted earring findings

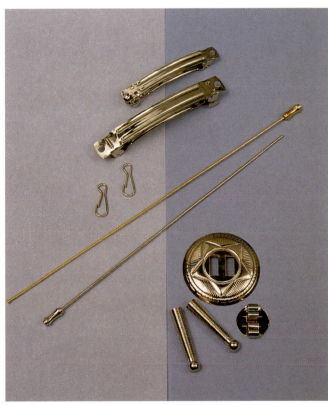

MISCELLANEOUS FINDINGS, TOP TO BOTTOM: Barrette backs, lanyard hooks, hat pins, bolo hardware

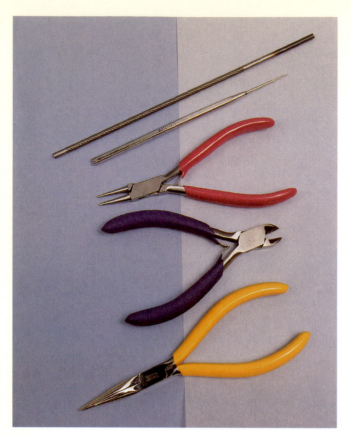

TOP TO BOTTOM: Wire file, awl, round-nose pliers, wire cutters, chain-nose pliers

Hammer and Anvil

Several projects in this book suggest the option of hammering your wire flat for a fashionable look. If you plan to use this technique often (and want a hammer with a good bit of force), consider investing in a ball peen hammer and an anvil (available in most bead stores). Otherwise, an ordinary household hammer will work fine. You also need a flat working surface that won't yield or chip.

Wire File

To shape the wire ends of projects such as the hair sticks on page 44, you'll need a wire file (available in any hardware store). A metal nail file also works well for most projects.

TECHNIQUES

Master some standard techniques, and you'll be able to tackle any of the projects in this book—and move on to many others.

Making a Wire Loop

Use this loop to attach any wired string of beads to almost anything else.

1. Use your chain-nose pliers to bend the wire to a right angle. If you're looping a piece of wire or a head pin that has already been strung with beads, be sure to leave enough room at the end for two or three wraps of wire (see Figure 10).

2. Grasp the wires near the right-angle bend with your round-nose pliers and, using your other hand, wrap the wire around the top jaw of the pliers (see Figure 11).

3. Reposition the pliers by removing them and reinserting them with the lower jaw inside the loop you've created. Use your other hand again to begin wrapping the wire (see Figure 12). The loop may be slightly off center. If so, use your pliers to center it over the beads.

4. Switch back to your chain-nose pliers. Hold the loop firmly and, with your other hand, wrap the wire around the neck of the loop until you almost reach the top bead. Keep the wire at a right angle as you wrap (see Figure 13).

5. Trim any remaining wire closely with wire cutters and tuck the end against the neck to prevent snagging.

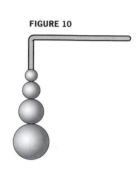

FIGURE 10

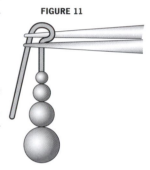

FIGURE 11

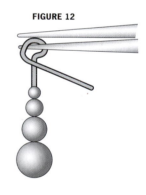

FIGURE 12

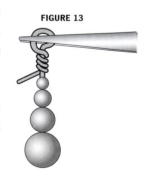

FIGURE 13

Making Fringe

Beads lend themselves beautifully to the flourish that fringe provides. Here's how to add movement to any border.

1. When you begin, your thread should be on a needle and anchored to the piece to which you are adding beaded fringe (such as the edge of a bookmark or the bottom of a pouch).

2. String beads to create the length of fringe you want. At the bottom, string a large bead to weight the fringe, followed by a small ending bead.

3. Thread through the small ending bead only once, then back up through all the other beads (see Figure 14).

4. Follow specific project instructions for continuing to add more fringe or tying off your thread.

FIGURE 14

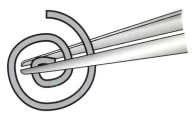

Making a Wire Spiral

This simple swirl gives you a decorative stopper at the end of a bead-filled wire.

1. Form a loop at the bottom of your wire with round-nose pliers.

2. Grasp the loop across its flat surface with chain-nose pliers and turn it sideways, coiling the wire around itself several times to create a spiral (see Figure 15).

3. Once finished, you may need to adjust the spiral to make sure it is centered on the wire.

FIGURE 15

A variety of metal beads

DESIGN BASICS

For each project in this book, you'll find step-by-step instructions illustrated by how-to photos and a detailed list of exactly what you need to create it. But don't forget, beads and beading are more art than science; don't panic if you can't find exactly the same wire basket as the one used in the charmed beaded basket project on page 60. Don't stop if your bottle doesn't look just like the one in the bath bottle project on page 54. And have no fear if you've got matte mauve beads—or even bright violet—instead of matte plum.

For some projects, such as the amulet pouch on page 28, the designer has spelled out the specifics involved in duplicating an intricate pattern or a distinct look. For other projects, it's best if you rejoice in the fact that you can't lay your hands on those same handmade beads from Africa or that exact style of ribbon. Use the need for substitution as an excuse to tap your creativity and sense of style.

Here are some design basics to help you improvise when you'd like.

Color

Designer Tracy Page Stilwell recommends you use an artist's color wheel (available for a few dollars in most art supply stores) as a visual guide and the world around you for inspiration.

"It's hard to go wrong if you stay in the same color family…for example, using many shades of blue, with one end of the blue scale going into purples and the other end going into green. Or, pair colors across from each other on the color wheel: yellow and purple, green and red, orange and blue. Also, flip through books and magazines to get ideas for color combinations you like, noticing everything from wallpaper to clothing. Colors that catch your eye can be translated into any medium."

—*Tracy Page Stilwell*

LYNN KRUCKE let the nature of her project direct her color choice when she used a mix of ocean-colored seed beads for this beaded fishbowl collar. To completely change the tone of the project, she suggests, simply change the color: "This would also be a great centerpiece for a bridal shower if done in whites and iridescent beads, with a floating candle or flowers in the water."

These pink vintage glass beads and blue crystal beads show the range of shades you can find within single colors.

Size and Shape

"Don't look for formulas—take risks and break the rules when working with combinations of sizes and shapes of beads. Consignment stores and moving sales can be wonderful and inexpensive sources of old jewelry, with interesting beads and findings that you can take apart and turn into something new and imaginative. Before you start a project, spread out your selection of beads and spend time working with different groupings of sizes and shapes to develop a style that is not only pleasing to you but that represents you as an individual. If you can't come up with the right arrangement of beads immediately, put your project away for a bit, focus on something else, then come back to it with a fresh perspective."

—*Susan Kinney*

These holiday ornaments show how the same basic idea can be carried out on different scales. **KÄTHE E. MOSER'S** sparkling tree and star feature large round beads collected in flea markets in India. In contrast, **JEAN PENLAND'S** delicate ornament designs are made with shimmering seed beads.

MELANIE ALTER uses beads in unexpected shapes and sizes to make simple pendants stand out. She says she scouts for beads everywhere: "I shop from catalogs, buy from people who make their own beads, and look for unusual bead stores that might sell old, locally made beads when I travel. I'm also finding that the large bead shows that are popping up in cities across the country are great sources for interesting pieces."

Texture and Character

"Experimenting with materials you don't usually work with or that you're not automatically drawn to is a great way to stimulate creativity. I also try to be observant of how other people combine beads and what choices they make in terms of materials and patterns. When you do that, you get your own ideas about how to achieve the look you want—or a new look. For example, I've started to combine my handmade beads with single colors of seed beads, silver accent beads, and simple components to give my work a very clean look. I have a friend, on the other hand, who mixes lots of gemstones, glass beads, and metal in random clusters for a much livelier effect."

—*Tracy Hildebrand*

Strung sea shells and dyed coconut shell.

LYNN KRUCKE chose beads that resemble lettered blocks to personalize this picture frame for her daughter.

BELOW: A stroll through the aisles of any respectable bead boutique will make it clear that shiny round balls are only the beginning of bead variety. Consider how beads that feature interesting surfaces, unusual materials, and novel designs can add to your project. This hand and turtle are carved bone; the fish is carnelian.

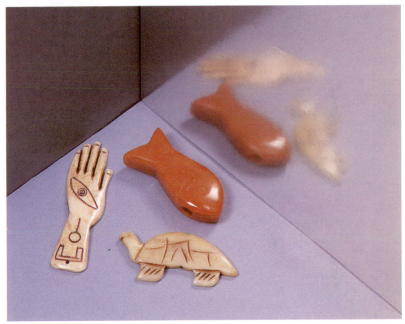

LEFT: Beads of carved clay and bone strung on raffia give SUSAN KINNEY'S paper-covered kaleidoscope an exotic feel. "If I had been trying to achieve a more modern look, I might have wrapped the kaleidoscope in gilding foil or even sprayed it with matte black, then used large, dramatic beads of metal or glass strung on colored wire—maybe even telephone wire—or thick, clear, plastic tubing. Or, for a more playful children's version, I think I would use primary colors for the background with a shiny finish glaze, then try twine, colored yarn, or patterned shoe laces to attach beads and buttons that represent a child's special interests, from ballerina shoes to little cars and animals."

Stringing Patterns

The projects in this book involve stringing beads onto thread, cord, wire, or findings. Figure 16 illustrates some common stringing approaches you can use, whether you're making a standard strung necklace or bracelet, creating fringe for a bookmark, or adding beads to a head pin that will dangle from a wire. If a project design calls for a random pattern but you'd like to try a repeating series with some favorite beads, experiment away! The chart in Figure 17 provides a guide for how many beads of various sizes you'll need for long strands.

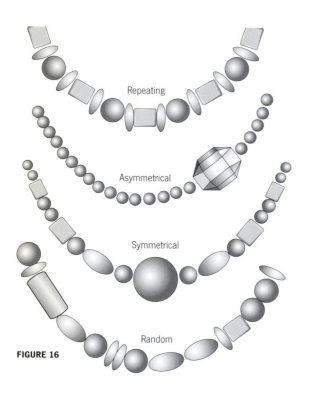

Repeating

Asymmetrical

Symmetrical

Random

FIGURE 16

JEAN PENLAND'S splendid strung necklaces show repeating, symmetrical, and random patterns.

This bracelet by **MELANIE ALTER** is a striking example of using a symmetrical focal point.

HOW MANY BEADS WILL YOU NEED?

BEAD SIZE	LENGTH OF STRAND		
	16 in. (41 cm)	18 in. (46.5 cm)	24 in. (61.5 cm)
4mm	100	112	153
6mm	68	76	100
8mm	50	56	76
10mm	40	45	61

FIGURE 17

TRACY HILDEBRAND adjusts the stringing pattern when she switches from a necklace (left) to a strand that will hold eye glasses.

Strung Necklace

DESIGN: **TRACY HILDEBRAND**

Get the hang of this basic design, and you can use it as a guide for making a multitude of strung necklaces. The Basics sections (pages 8–23) outline all the elements, from clasps to common designs, that you'll need to build on this theme.

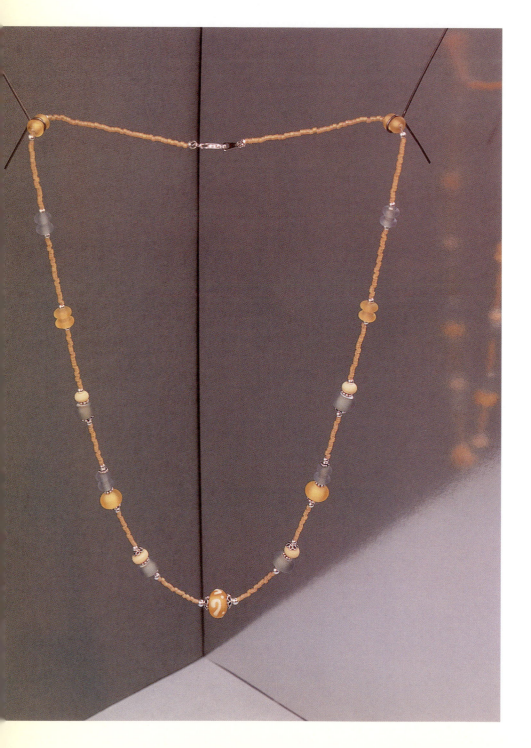

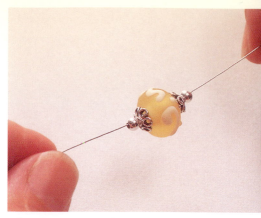

1 Center your focal bead on the wire. Frame each side of the focal bead with a bead cap and a round silver bead.

YOU WILL NEED

Approximately 26 inches (67 cm) of .012 diameter flexible beading wire (To make a necklace of another length, simply cut your wire 2 to 3 inches [5–8 cm] longer than you want the necklace to be.)

Approximately 20 handmade glass beads, including one focal bead

Approximately 1 tablespoon of size 11 seed beads in an accent color

Assortment of 2.5 and 3mm round sterling silver beads

Assortment of silver bead caps and spacers

2 silver bead tips

12mm flat lobster claw clasp and chain tag

Round-nose pliers

Tape

Bead cement

Needle or toothpick

HOW TO

Bead Tips, page 13

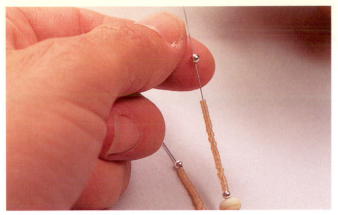

2 Slide on approximately 1 inch (2.5 cm) of seed beads, followed by a grouping of two glass beads, each framed by a round silver bead and a bead cap and separated by a spacer. After completing a section on one side of the focal bead, string an identical section on the other side, and compare the two sides for evenness before moving on. About halfway up the necklace, begin stringing only one glass bead framed by round silver beads at each interval.

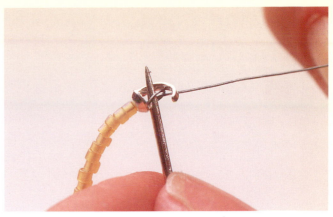

3 Once you've finished stringing beads, tape one end of thread to keep the beads from sliding off. On the other end, string on a bead tip and knot the wire as close to the tip as possible. Knot the wire again, and use a needle or toothpick to dot each knot with bead cement and poke the knots down into the bead tip.

4 With round-nose pliers, attach the tail of the bead tip to the lobster claw clasp and close it.

5 Remove the tape, knot a bead tip onto the other end of the string, and attach it to the chain tag.

VARIATION

Experiment with finishing your necklace ends with crimp beads rather than bead tips (see Crimp Beads, page 13). Also, try other clasps or even spectacle ends (available where findings are sold) to turn the necklace into a string for eye glasses.

Knotted Cord Necklace

DESIGN: **MELANIE ALTER**

The materials list is short and the process unbelievably simple—with spectacular results. What makes this necklace such a work of art is the stunning combination of bold and unusual beads strung together in a striking fashion. Prowl among the collections of exotic ethnic beads in boutiques and mail-order catalogs to find beads similar to the ones featured in this design. Soon, you'll begin spotting one-of-a-kind finds that lend themselves to your own variations on this necklace theme.

YOU WILL NEED

4 feet (122 cm) of leather cord

1 large stone doughnut bead

1 silver cone (with hole large enough to accommodate doubled cord)

1 semiprecious barrel bead (with hole large enough to accommodate doubled cord)

2 decorative silver spacers

1 String the large doughnut bead onto the center of your cord.

2 Make sure the ends of the cord are even, then string the silver cone on top of the doughnut bead. Finally, add the barrel bead.

3 Secure the beads in place with a firm knot positioned snugly against the barrel bead.

4 Knot one end of the cord approximately 2½ inches (6.5 cm) from the end. Add one of the decorative spacers, and knot the cord on the other side of the spacer to hold it in place.

5 Repeat the process of knotting around a decorative spacer on the second end of the cord.

VARIATION

Other types of cord also work with this design. Waxed linen cord comes in a variety of colors. So does rattail, which has a satin-like appearance that creates a dressier look.

Amulet Pouch

DESIGN: **CAROLE TRIPP**

Enchanting little necklace bags like these (perfect for carrying everything from crystals to small lipsticks) are wildly popular. Trouble is, most designs require that you know how to bead weave if you want to make them yourself—and few bead weaving techniques lend themselves to weekend mastery. But with this imaginative design, you can achieve the look you're after with the simplest of standard sewing stitches.

5 inches (13 cm) of ribbon 2 inches (5 cm) wide (If your ribbon has a pattern, take note of the motif you want at the center of the pouch; you may need to start with a bit more ribbon to have a central part of the pattern on the front of your pouch.)

1 yard (.95 m) of 2 to 3mm twisted or plain rattail

Beading thread to blend with your ribbon

Beading needle

Liquid seam sealant or glue

Straight pins

4 to 5 grams of size 11 seed beads (gray-lined clear aurora borealis)

1 gram size 11 seed beads (gunmetal)

3 4mm Montana blue diamond-shaped Austrian crystals

5 5mm Montana blue diamond-shaped Austrian crystals

1 6mm Montana blue diamond-shaped Austrian crystal

11 5x7mm crystal with silver ovals

12 4mm Montana blue smooth rondell-shaped glass beads

13 4mm light pink smooth rondell-shaped glass beads

1 4mm light gunmetal smooth rondell-shaped glass bead

12 6mm light pink matte faceted fire polish glass beads

1 6mm Montana blue faceted fire polish glass bead

4 4mm Montana blue faceted fire polish glass beads

2 5x7mm light pink twisted ovals

11 7x10mm Austrian crystal drops

1 8x12mm Austrian crystal drop

6 3x5mm light pink ovals (egglets)

HOW TO

Making Fringe, page 17

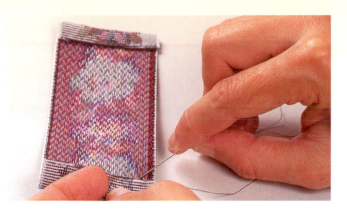

1 Decide on your pouch's front motif (such as the rose on this design) and center it by folding the ribbon in half. The fold will be the bottom of the pouch. Allowing ¼ to ½ inch (1 to 1.5 cm) at the top edges for a hem, cut the ribbon. Using liquid seam sealant or white glue, finish the two cut edges by applying a thin line of either substance. Let the hems dry 15 to 30 minutes, then fold over the hem allowance to the wrong side and stitch it in place, making sure the stitches don't show on the outside of the pouch.

2 You will use a diagonal whipstitch to stitch together the two side edges of the pouch, adding a gray-lined clear seed bead to each stitch (see Figure 1).

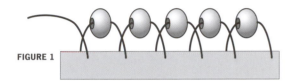

FIGURE 1

To begin, fold the pouch so the two hems meet at the top and the wrong sides are together. Use a pin or two to hold the pouch together and make the stitching easier. Begin at the top edge of one side. Bury your end knot in the hem. Take one stitch directly across the top edge and come back through at the starting point without adding a bead. Then, begin your diagonal stitch, adding a bead with each stitch. As you sew, make sure the travel part of your stitch goes diagonally down along the outside edge of the pouch and the stitching

part goes diagonally up through the ribbon. Place your stitches about 1 bead length apart. The beads should sit so that the hole is not visible from the front or back. Finish off the first side by tying a knot and burying the tail inside. Begin the second side at  the top as well. When you complete the second side, do not tie off and cut your thread; you will use this thread to appliqué a row of beads along the bottom edge. (Hint: to make the last bead on the first side line up, come out at the bottom corner of the pouch, then thread your needle up through 4 or 5 beads. Knot off the thread and tuck it to the inside.)

FIGURE 2

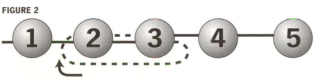

3 To appliqué the beads along the bottom fold, begin with your thread coming out of the bottom corner of the fold. Put three beads on the needle and slide them down the base of the thread. Lay them along the bottom fold and insert your needle into the fold after the third bead. Come back out between the first bead and the second bead. Pass the needle through the second and third beads and add 2 more beads (see Figure 2). Go into the fabric where these two beads end and come up between the second and third beads. Pass the needle through the third, fourth and fifth beads and add 2 more beads. Continue in this manner until you have appliquéd a row of beads along the bottom fold of the pouch. In this design, with a ribbon width of 2 inches (5 cm), 31 beads have been appliquéd across the bottom.

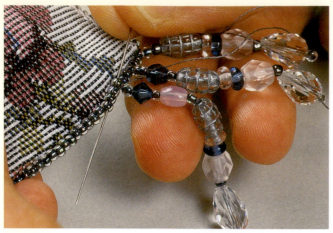

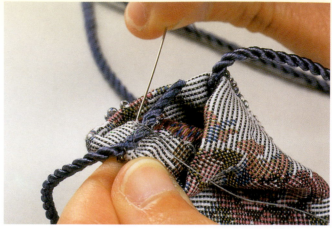

4 The fringe will hang off the appliquéd beads and should be evenly distributed. With 31 appliquéd beads, the fringe will hang on the following beads: 1, 4, 7, 10, 13, 16, 19, 22, 25, 28, 31 (see Figure 3).

5 To attach the cord for the neck chain, determine the length you want your pouch necklace to be. The ends of the cord will extend into the bag about 1 inch (2.5 cm). Before attaching the cord to the pouch, finish the ends to prevent fraying or unraveling by applying liquid seam sealant or white glue to each end and allowing it to dry 15 to 30 minutes. Insert one end of the cord into the pouch and hold it against one side. Stitch the cord to the inside of the pouch, using a whipstitch over the cord and passing through the cord every few stitches so it lies against the side beads. Check for length once more to be sure you're satisfied before stitching the second end.

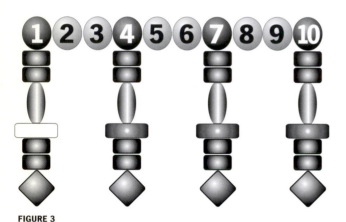

FIGURE 3

When attaching the fringe, your needle will come out one side of the bead on which the fringe is to hang, go through the beads on the fringe once, come back up through the beads (skipping the final seed bead), and go in on the other side of the bead on which it hangs (see Making Fringe, page 17). After finishing a strand, go through the next 2 seed beads to be in position for the next strand.

Create your fringe according to the Fringe Pattern on page 31.

Once you have added all of the fringe, tie a knot around one of the threads and tuck the end into the inside.

Some of Carole Tripp's other amulet pouch designs are featured on page 50.

VARIATIONS

6 You'll make a final piece of fringe with dual strands at the top for the closure drop. Begin at the center of the back of the pouch. Bury your knot in the top fold, and add the following beads to your needle: 17 gray-lined clear seed beads, 1 light pink oval, 1 gray-lined clear seed bead, 1 6mm blue diamond-shaped crystal, 1 pink rondell, 1 blue rondell, 1 6mm pink matte round, 1 gunmetal seed bead, 1 7x10mm crystal drop, 1 gray-lined clear seed bead. Skip the last seed bead and go back up through the rest of the beads, including the light pink oval, but not the 17 seed beads. Add 17 more gray-lined clear seed beads to create your second strand. Go back into the top fold and knot off your thread.

FRINGE PATTERN:

STRAND #1: 1 gray-lined clear seed bead, 1 gunmetal seed bead, 1 crystal with silver oval, 1 pink rondell, 1 blue rondell, 1 6mm pink matte round, 1 gunmetal seed bead, 1 7x10mm crystal drop, 1 gray-lined clear seed bead

STRAND #2: 2 gray-lined clear seed beads, 1 4mm blue fire polish, 1 gray-lined clear seed bead, 1 crystal with silver oval, 1 pink rondell, 1 blue rondell, 1 6mm pink matte round, 1 gunmetal seed bead, 1 7x10mm crystal drop, 1 gray-lined clear seed bead

STRAND #3: 1 gray-lined clear seed bead, 1 4mm blue diamond-shaped crystal, 1 gray-lined clear seed bead, 1 pink oval, 1 gray-lined clear seed bead, 1 crystal with silver oval, 1 pink rondell, 1 blue rondell, 1 6mm pink matte round, 1 gunmetal seed bead, 1 7x10mm crystal drop, 1 gray-lined clear seed bead

STRAND #4: 1 gray-lined clear seed bead, 1 gunmetal seed bead, 1 gray-lined clear seed bead, 1 pink twisted oval, 1 gray-lined clear seed bead, 1 5mm blue diamond-shaped crystal, 1 gray-lined clear seed bead, 1 crystal with silver oval, 1 pink rondell, 1 blue rondell, 1 6mm pink matte round, 1 gunmetal seed bead, 1 7x10mm crystal drop, 1 gray-lined clear seed bead

STRAND #5: 2 gray-lined clear seed beads, 1 gunmetal seed bead, 1 gray-lined clear seed bead, 1 4mm blue fire polish, 1 gray-lined clear seed bead, 1 pink oval, 1 gray-lined clear seed bead, 1 5mm blue diamond-shaped crystal, 1 gray-lined clear seed bead, 1 pink oval, 1 gray-lined clear seed bead, 1 5mm blue diamond-shaped crystal, 1 gray-lined clear seed bead, 1 crystal with silver oval, 1 pink rondell, 1 blue rondell, 1 6mm pink matte round, 1 gunmetal seed bead, 1 7x10mm crystal drop, 1 gray-lined clear seed bead

STRAND #6: 2 gray-lined clear seed beads, 1 4mm blue diamond-shaped crystal, 1 gray-lined clear seed bead, 1 pink oval, 1 gray-lined clear seed bead, 1 5mm blue diamond-shaped crystal, 1 gray-lined clear seed bead, 1 crystal with silver oval, 1 pink rondell, 1 6mm blue fire polish, 1 pink rondell, 1 blue rondell, 1 6mm pink matte round, 1 gunmetal rondell, 1 8x12mm crystal drop, 1 gray-lined clear seed bead

STRAND #7: repeat strand #5

STRAND #8: repeat strand #4

STRAND #9: repeat strand #3

STRAND #10: repeat strand #2

STRAND #11: repeat strand #1

Memory Wire Bracelet

DESIGN: **MELANIE ALTER**

The bundles-of-bangles look is big. With memory wire, you can create a clever variation—a bunch of bracelets all in one. Widely available in bead and craft stores, memory wire remains coiled even after you've beaded it and wrapped it around your wrist. The spiral shape lends itself especially well to funky ethnic finds, like the beads and charms featured in this design.

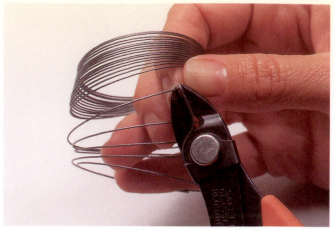

1 Cut the wire so that you're working with a length that forms three complete and two half loops.

YOU WILL NEED

Memory wire

A handful (literally) of assorted large-holed ethnic beads
(In the design shown, Melanie Alter has used a variety of tube- and barrel-shaped African beads of horn and dyed bone, some glass beads, chips, and tiny bronze spacers.)

Charms
(a variety of bronze charms are used in this design)

Jump rings (optional)

Round-nose pliers

Chain-nose pliers

Wire cutters

HOW TO

Jump Rings, page 14 (optional)

Making a Wire Loop, page 16 (optional)

2 With the round-nose pliers, form a loop at one
end of the wire to keep the beads you will string
from falling off.

3 String beads and charms onto the wire in a
random fashion. Be sure the beads you've chosen
have large enough holes; don't force small-holed beads
onto the wire. As you work, check to see that the beads
lie next to each other well. Large beads on adjacent
coils will likely crowd each other and prevent the coils
from lying smoothly.

4 Most charms have loops that can be strung onto
the wire along with the beads. If you've chosen
some charms without loops (or if the loops are too
small to string), simply make your own or use a jump
ring. (See Making a Wire Loop, page 16, or Jump
Rings, page 14.)

5 When you've filled the wire with charms and
beads, add a final charm and use the round-nose
pliers to form a closing loop.

VARIATIONS

Some of Melanie Alter's other memory wire bracelet
designs are featured on page 49.

1 Begin slipping beads and spacers onto the elastic in an alternating pattern.

Stretch Bracelet

DESIGN: **MELANIE ALTER**

Simple, chic bracelets like this one are hard to resist. Fortunately, they're also easy to create. With elastic as your stringing material, beads and baubles of all shapes and sizes will cling elegantly to your wrist.

YOU WILL NEED

Approximately 9 inches (23 cm) of 1/16-inch (1.5-mm) elastic cord in a color that matches or complements your beads (gold is used in this design)

Approximately 12 14–16mm large-holed glass beads (handmade amber-colored beads are used in this design)

Approximately 11 spacers in a metal that complements the beads (bronze spacers are used in this design)

Large charm

Jump ring (optional)

Bead cement

Needle, straight pin, or toothpick

HOW TO

Jump Rings, page 14 (optional)

Making a Wire Loop, page 16 (optional)

VARIATIONS

Some of Melanie Alter's other stretch bracelet designs are featured on page 50.

2 After stringing all the beads and spacers, add a single charm. You can either string the charm directly onto the elastic, create a wire loop, or use a jump ring so that the charm dangles from the elastic. (See Jump Rings, page 14, or Making a Wire Loop, page 16.)

3 This project design is for a standard-size bracelet; it should fit snugly on most wrists. However, if you're making the bracelet for your own wrist (or for another wrist that happens to be nearby), you can test the size before knotting the elastic. Make sure it's tight enough so that it won't slip off. If necessary, trim the elastic slightly.

4 Once you're satisfied with the size, knot the elastic.

5 With a needle, straight pin, or toothpick, dot the knot with bead cement. Once the cement is dry (approximately 15 minutes), push the knot into the nearest bead hole.

Drop Earrings

DESIGN: **LINDA ROSE NALL**

This classic design incorporates two of the most common wire-wrapping techniques to create beaded dangles that hang from purchased ear wires. Once you have the knack of making these (almost) instant earrings, you may not stop until you've created a pair to match every color and style in your wardrobe.

1 Cut a 6-inch (15-cm) piece of wire. Make a loop (see Making a Wire Loop, page 16) at one end.

YOU WILL NEED

16–18 inches (41-46 cm) of 22-gauge sterling silver wire

4 amber chip beads

2 5mm round amethyst beads

2 painted wooden focal beads

1 pair of silver ear wires

Round-nose pliers

Chain-nose pliers

Wire cutters

Jewelry hammer and anvil (optional)

HOW TO

Making a Wire Loop, page 16

Making a Wire Spiral, page 17

VARIATIONS

Some of Linda Rose Nall's other drop earring designs are featured on page 48.

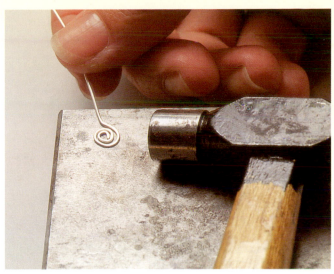

2 String an amber chip bead, a focal bead, and a second amber chip bead. Make a second wire loop at the top of the wire to hold the beads in place.

3 Cut a 2-inch (5-cm) piece of wire. Create a spiral at one end (see Making a Wire Spiral, page 17). To achieve a contemporary look, gently flatten the spiral using a jewelry hammer and anvil.

4 Add an amethyst bead above the spiral, and use a wire loop at the top to attach this second piece to the base of the earring.

5 Repeat steps 1–4 to create your second earring, with the spiral on the second earring twisting in the opposite direction from the spiral on the first. Attach both earrings to ear wires. To make sure the lengths of your earrings are even, hold the earrings together before making the loop at the bottom of the base of the second earring. Once you've finished both earrings, you may need to adjust the wire slightly with chain-nose pliers to make sure it's straight and that all of the loops are hanging in the appropriate direction.

Wire Hoop Earrings

DESIGN: **KIMBERLEY ADAMS**

Master this uncomplicated process for making one of the most popular earring styles selling, and you'll be wearing nothing but your own creations from now on. In the design shown, Kimberely Adams has used her own handmade beads (made of amber glass) as focal beads for the earrings. Warning: ferreting out new focal beads for "just one more pair" may become an all-consuming passion.

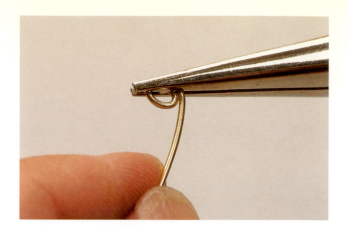

1 Cut a piece of wire about 6 inches (15.5 cm) long to wire your focal bead. Make a spiral on one end (see Making a Wire Spiral, page 17).

YOU WILL NEED

Approximately 20 inches (51 cm) of 20-gauge gold wire

2 focal beads

10 size 6 seed beads in color to complement focal bead

10 size 8 seed beads in color to complement focal bead and contrast with the other seed beads

Round-nose pliers

Chain-nose pliers

Spool (with or without thread)

HOW TO

Making a Wire Spiral, page 17

Making a Wire Loop, page 16

2 Add the focal bead, one size 6 seed bead, and one size 8 seed bead, and secure them with a loop on top (see Making a Wire Loop, page 16).

3 Cut a 4-inch (10.5-cm) piece of wire for the hoop. Use the spool as a form to shape the piece into a circle. With round-nose pliers, make a loop at one end, then adjust the loop slightly to make sure it's centered over the rest of the wire.

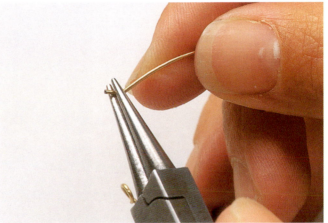

4 From the other end, string on two size 8 beads, two size 6 beads, the focal bead, two size 6 beads, and two size 8 beads.

5 Using chain-nose pliers, bend the other end of the wire at a right angle. Hook the bent end into the loop to close the earring. Repeat the process for the second earring.

Handmade Pin

DESIGN: **TRACY HILDEBRAND**

While giant safety pins are widely available wherever jewelry findings are sold, it's a simple (and rewarding) matter to twist your own out of a nickel hat pin. Add some distinctive beads (Tracy Hildebrand made her own for this design), and the result is a sharp accessory to hang on everything from vests to coats.

YOU WILL NEED

1 10-inch (26-cm) nickel hat pin

2 to 4 3mm sterling silver round beads

5 to 7 sterling silver wire coil beads

Several sterling silver bead caps

Assorted 3 to 10mm glass beads

Round-nose pliers

Chain-nose pliers

Wire cutters

HOW TO

Making a Wire Loop, page 16

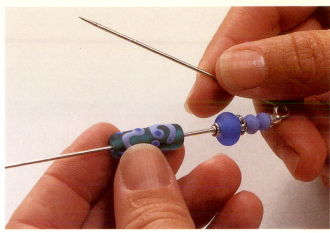

1 Grasp the hat pin with the round-nose pliers 2½ inches (6.5 cm) from the sharp end of the pin. With your fingers, wrap the blunt end of the pin around the widest part of the pliers nose twice so that both ends of the wire are facing the same direction.

2 Slide the beads onto the blunt end of the pin. Play with various arrangements until you achieve a look you like, using silver beads as spacers between glass beads. Your grouping of beads should be about 1½ inches (4 cm) long.

3 Using the pliers, grasp the blunt end of the pin about ¾ inch (2 cm) from the last bead, then, using your fingers, bend it around the small end of the pliers nose. Press the loop tightly with your pliers.

4 Bend the pin again about ⅛ inch (.5 cm) from the last bead, and loop the wire back on itself until the last wrap rests against the ending bead (see Making a Wire Loop, page 16). Trim any excess wire.

5 Grasp the flat loop at its middle and bend it around the pliers to make a hook. Holding the pin so that the pointed end is at the top, bend the entire hook at a 90-degree angle to the beads and fit the pointed end under the hook.

YOU WILL NEED

1 2-inch (5-cm) sterling silver head pin

2 sterling silver bead caps

1 3mm sterling silver round bead

1 large glass focal bead, approximately ¾ inch (2 cm) long

1 sterling silver split jump ring

1 10mm lobster claw clasp

Round-nose pliers

Chain-nose pliers

Wire cutters

HOW TO

Jump Rings, page 14

Making a Wire Loop, page 16

VARIATION

Feel free to experiment with various bead sizes and combinations. Just remember, if you use larger beads, you may need a longer head pin.

Zipper Pull

DESIGN: **TRACY HILDEBRAND**

With a sterling silver head pin and that brilliant bead you've been saving to show off, you can create this clever clip-on piece. It's an imaginative way to jazz up a jacket—plus, it does double duty. A quick switch changes the piece from zipper pull to pendant.

1 Slide the beads onto the head pin in the order shown (bead cap, focal bead, bead cap, round bead).

2 Make a loop with the remaining wire on the head pin (see Making a Wire Loop, page 16).

3 Attach the split jump ring to the loop (see Jump Rings, page 14).

4 Use the split jump ring to attach the zipper pull to the lobster claw clasp, and clip the clasp to the hole on a zipper.

5 Turn your zipper pull into a pendant by replacing the split jump ring and lobster claw clasp with a bail (available where jewelry findings are sold) that can snap onto the wire loop and then connect directly to a chain.

Hair Sticks

DESIGN: **KERRI SULLIVAN**

Bind a few beautiful beads with some twists and turns of wire, and you'll never again have a moment's peace in the front row of the movie theatre or at the head of the grocery check-out line. "Excuse me," the question starts. "Where can I find one of those?"

1 Slide your first bead onto the wire, about 6 inches (15 cm) from one end. With chain-nose pliers, kink the wire slightly, just below the bead, to hold it in place.

YOU WILL NEED

18 inches (46 cm) of
16-gauge silver wire

3 handmade beads with large holes

Round-nose pliers

Chain-nose pliers

Wire cutters

Wire file

Jewelry hammer and anvil (optional)

HOW TO

Making a Wire Spiral, page 17

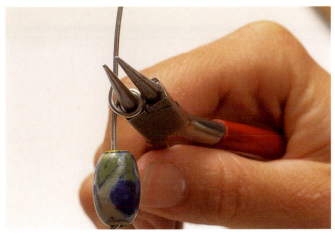

2 Switch to round-nose pliers and twist a loop above the first bead, then add a second bead.

3 After the second bead, twist the wire into a spiral (see Making a Wire Spiral, page 17).

4 Add the third bead, and kink the wire as you did underneath the first bead to hold it in place.

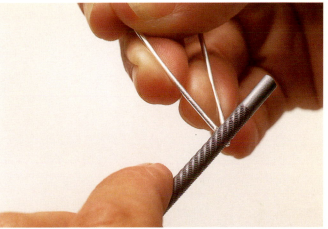

5 Cut the ends of the wire, if necessary, so that the bottoms of the sticks are even. For an especially contemporary look, use a jewelry hammer and anvil to flatten the sticks. Simply lay them on the anvil and gently pound them to about half their rounded thickness. Smooth and round the ends with a wire file.

Rainbow Baseball Cap

DESIGN: **TRACY PAGE STILWELL**

You'll be the belle of the ball game in this rainbow-studded cap. The combination of brightly colored bugles on classic black cries out for dark glasses—and perhaps a pair of designer sneakers.

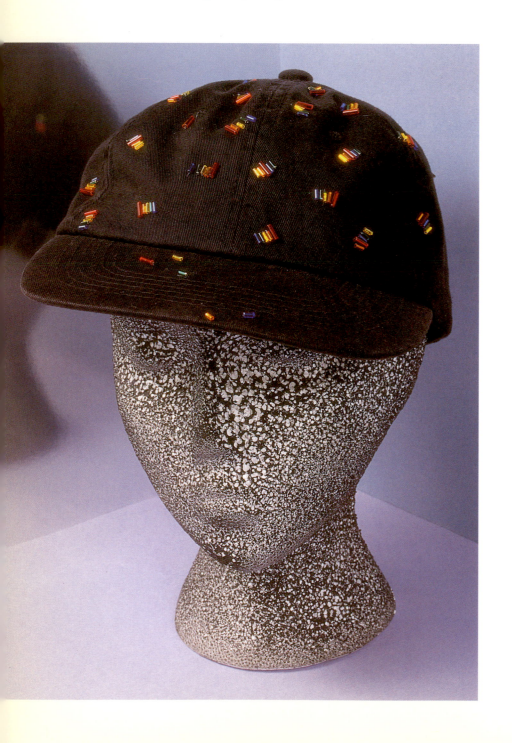

VARIATION

Experiment with other hat and bead colors. A gradation of colors—maybe powder to midnight blue on a white hat, for example—would be striking.

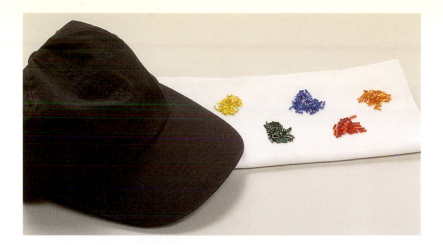

1 Spread out a towel and separate your beads into colored piles on the towel.

2 With a pencil, lightly mark spots around the cap where you plan to sew bead clusters. The clusters should be scattered around the entire cap (except for the bill) and be approximately 1 to 1½ inches (2.5 to 4 cm) apart.

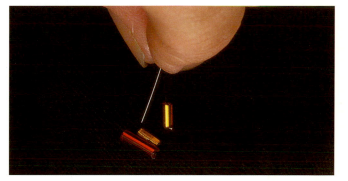

3 Thread your needle, knot the end, and, at one of the spots you've marked, come up through the inside of the cap. Begin sewing clusters of the five colors of beads on, one bead at a time, by passing your needle and thread through each bead and back into the cap. Each time you add a bead in a cluster, start your new stitch close against the beginning of the stitch you've just completed.

4 After finishing a cluster of five beads, come up through the inside of the cap at a nearby spot you've marked and begin a new cluster. You can vary both the order of the colors and the position of the beads in each cluster.

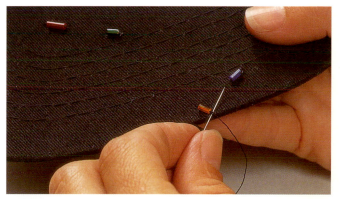

5 Sew one bead of each color in a random pattern onto the topside of the brim. Hide your starting knot in the seam where the cap and the brim meet. After sewing on your last bead, come back up through the fabric and knot your thread off on your final stitch.

GALLERY OF JEWELRY AND ACCESSORIES

ABOVE: If you've already settled on the dramatic effect of a hat, don't stop there. Slide a few showy beads onto a hat pin, secure them with a crimp bead, and sashay off in complete style.

KERRI SULLIVAN AND BARBARA WRIGHT

RIGHT: An arrangement of a few bright beads sets off these wooden hair sticks. With hair sticks with pre-drilled holes, it's an easy matter of inserting a beaded head pin (sand the end first and dip it in glue) to create a distinctive accessory.

TRACY HILDEBRAND

RIGHT: A few examples of the abundant options for adapting the basic drop earring design on page 36. **TRACY HILDEBRAND** (pair on left) incorporated her own handmade beads. **LINDA ROSE NALL** used semiprecious stones.

LEFT: These spectacular variations on the theme show a variety of approaches to the memory wire bracelet project on page 32.

MELANIE ALTER

BELOW: This bag's checkerboard pattern provides the perfect backdrop for stitching a handful of handsome buttons and beads. The carved bone, metal, and whimsical shapes are an ideal match for the textured fabric.

MELANIE ALTER

LEFT: This under-the-arm purse by designer **NANCY MCGAHA** was a place mat in a former life. She folded it in thirds, sewed the sides of the bottom fold, and attached beads and trinkets to the top flap, using a few focal beads as anchors and highlighting the scallops she created by knotting portions of the fringe.

With distinctive beads and interesting charms, **MELANIE ALTER** shows ways to vary the stretch braclet design on page 34.

LEFT: CAROLE TRIPP'S variations of her amulet pouch (page 28), and a needle-woven necklace with beads by fiber artist **HELEN BANES**.

LEFT: A splashy silver array of jingling beads and charms is the perfect accent for the ethnic style of this handmade vest.

MELANIE ALTER

RIGHT: This assortment of jewelry from **TRACY HILDEBRAND**'s classy collection illustrates the use of a variety of clasps and findings.

Napkin Rings

DESIGN: **KIMBERLEY ADAMS**

It's hard to imagine more distinctive table decorations. Once you've mastered the pattern below, personalize the process to adorn every holiday table in need of decor—and suit every food lover you know. How about beads of glittering silver and gold for Christmas? Red, white, and blue rings are an ideal accent for summer picnics. You can even match your beads to the bride's china for a shower gift that's sure to stand out.

1 Kink your wire at one end to prevent the beads from falling off, leaving a tail of approximately 1 inch (2.5 cm). Begin stringing your base-color beads in an alternating pattern.

YOU WILL NEED

Assortment of size 6 seed beads (approximately 1½ heaping tablespoons per napkin ring) in colors to complement your napkins (In the napkin rings shown, Kimberley Adams has alternated iridescent matte topaz and gunmetal on the base and used black as a contrasting color on the twisted strands.)

1 39-inch (100-cm) piece of 20-gauge copper wire per napkin ring

Round-nose pliers

Chain-nose pliers

Wire cutters

2 Once you have strung about 6 inches (15 cm) worth of beads (approximately 60 beads), twist the beaded section into a loop. Secure the loop by using round-nose pliers to twist the tail you left around the main piece of wire. After securing the loop, clip any excess wire from the tail with wire cutters.

3 Make three more 6-inch (15-cm) sections in the same alternating pattern of beads. Twist each section into a loop as you complete it. You do not need to secure these loops.

4 After the final loop, string the rest of the wire with your contrasting bead color, kink the end to hold the beads on the wire, and wrap the beaded wire around the four loops.

5 When you've finished wrapping the loops, use chain-nose pliers to twist the end of the wire around a piece of wire on the napkin ring. Clip any excess wire with wire cutters.

VARIATION

For an even bolder look, you can experiment with beads that are larger in size. Just be sure to use a slightly longer piece of wire if you do, and make your loops a bit larger.

1 Knot the ends of your strand of beads together so it forms a circle, and loosely wrap it around the bottle neck several times.

YOU WILL NEED

1 large bottle with an interesting shape (can be clear, colored, or frosted), filled with a favorite bath product

1 cork stopper

Approximately 2 feet (62 cm) of 20- to 24-gauge gold or silver wire

A strand of small beads approximately 12 inches (31 cm) long (Many kinds of beads can be purchased in strands in bead stores; Susan Kinney used small, iridescent purple hearts.)

Approximately 3 dozen assorted glass beads in complementary colors and contrasting shapes and sizes, including a variety of seed beads

6 to 8 assorted metal beads

6 to 8 head pins

Chain-nose pliers

Round-nose pliers

HOW TO

Making a Wire Spiral, page 17

Bath Bottle

DESIGN: SUSAN KINNEY

Think Neptunian colors of sea green and marine when you're shopping for these bottles and beads. Designer Susan Kinney has used head pins and gold wire to wrap the neck of a bath salt bottle in a shimmering array of beads. Variations on the theme are plentiful, from bottles of bubble bath strung with shells to bath oil wrapped with bright wooden beads carved in the shapes of fish.

2 Cut two lengths of wire, each approximately 10 inches (26 cm) long. Wrap each around and between the string of beads on the bottle neck, leaving two 3- to 4-inch (8- to 10-cm) tails on either side.

3 Create dangles by adding an assortment of beads in a random fashion to the head pins, stringing the beads against the flat end "stopper." Leave approximately ½ inch (1.5 cm) at the other end; in the next step, you will loop this end around the wire to attach the dangles to the bottle.

4 Lay your dangles out together to make sure you like the variety of designs you've created. Once you're satisfied, add three dangles to one side of the bottle neck by using your chain-nose pliers to create a small loop at the end opposite each head pin's flat end. Twist each loop over one of the 3- to 4-inch (8- to 10-cm) wire tails you created and pinch it gently into place. When all three dangles on one side are attached, twist the wire tail around itself just above the bunch of dangle loops to hold them in place, then clip the excess wire. Repeat the process on the other side of the bottle neck.

5 You should have one remaining wire tail on each side of the bottle neck. Add several beads to each tail and create a spiral at the end to hold them in place and add design interest (see Making a Wire Spiral, page 17).

VARIATIONS

Painted Box

DESIGN: **ALLISON STILWELL**

*This catchy container has folk-art flair. Create bright and whimsical
accessories just like it with a box of cardboard or papier-mâché
and some fanciful embellishments that can frolic on its lid.*

YOU WILL NEED

Papier-mâché or cardboard box

Acrylic paint in light periwinkle,
orchid, and lime

Beading thread

Beading needle

Several tablespoons of size 8 seed
beads in a variety of colors

Bead cement

Paintbrush

Scissors

Awl

Pencil

1 Paint the bottom of the box with one coat of
periwinkle and the top with one coat of orchid
(you may want to use two coats if your paint is light or
your surface is especially absorbent). Once the paint is
dry (about an hour), sketch small triangles in a random design on the lid and paint them in lime. Paint
thin stripes of lime in ½-inch (1.5-cm) intervals
around the rim of the lid.

2 At the three points on every painted triangle and
in between each of the stripes on the rim, make
tiny holes with the awl.

3 Cut a piece of thread 12 to 15 inches (31 to 38.5 cm) long. Knot a bead to one end of the thread, thread your needle on the other end, and pull the thread through one of the holes around the design until it is stopped by the knotted bead.

4 String enough beads in random color patterns to reach the next hole in the triangle you are working on, then pass the needle down through that hole. Come up through the next closest hole and continue. After completing a triangle, move on (from the underneath side) to the next one until every triangle has a beaded border. If the thread starts to get short, tie it off with a knot on the underneath side, add a drop of bead cement to the knot, and begin a new thread as outlined in step 3.

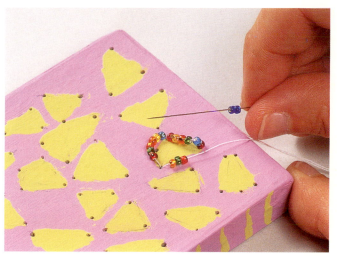

5 To attach beads to the rim, pass your needle through the hole from the inside, thread a bead, then come back through the hole and move on to the next one. When you've finished with the rim, knot your thread and add a drop of bead cement.

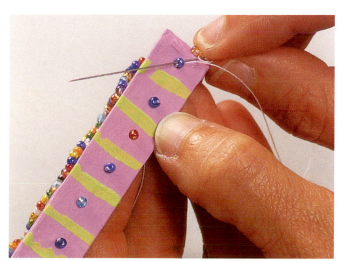

VARIATION

If you're beading borders that are longer, curved, or more intricate, you may want to anchor your beaded strands with some additional stitches. Poke holes at more frequent intervals than you did with the three points of each triangle. After stringing beads along one edge of a border, come up through your starting hole, pass your thread between two beads in the first section of the border, and go back down through the next hole. Continue traveling in this fashion to secure the beaded strands (see Figure 1).

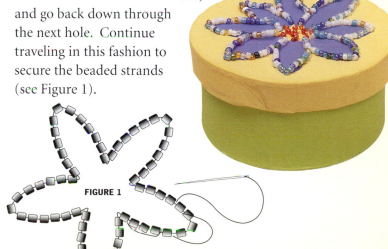

FIGURE 1

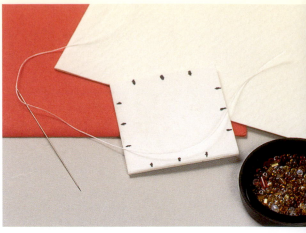

1 Measure ½ teaspoon of each color of the beads you have chosen to work with into your small container and set them aside. Measure a 1½ inch (4 cm) square onto your cardboard or mat board and cut it out. Make your grid template by marking ⅜-inch (1-cm) intervals around the perimeter of the square.

Beaded Greeting Card

DESIGN: **TERRY B. TAYLOR**

Your correspondence will never be ho-hum again. Tailor your color scheme to the holiday or season—soft pastels at Easter or maybe shades of amber and russet in the fall. It takes no time to produce a handmade card for a last-minute occasion. And if you feel ambitious some rainy weekend, settle in with a supply of multicolored seed beads and a stash of pretty paper to create a stockpile of birthday cards that will last for months to come.

YOU WILL NEED

Blank greeting card (purchase one or make your own from decorative paper)

Small scrap of cardboard or mat board

Ruler

Scissors

Pencil

Magazine

Sewing needle or awl

Beading needle

Bead thread

Transparent tape

Assorted seed beads in complementary colors and a small, flat container (a jar lid works well)

Decorative paper (paper can match your card or accent your bead colors)

Glue

Small piece of wax paper

2 Open the card and lay it on the magazine. Position your template on the card and use the awl to prick holes in the card, following the marked spaces on your template.

3 Thread the beading needle and pass it from the inside of the card to the front through one of the pricked holes. Secure the end of the thread with tape. Begin to randomly pick up beads with your needle until you have enough to cover the thread from one hole to the hole directly across the grid (you'll use approximately 20 beads per row). Bring the thread through to the back, then move to the next hole.

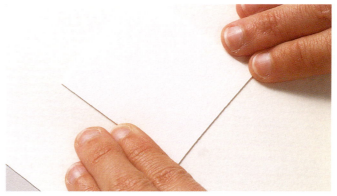

4 Work all of the vertical rows first, then all of the horizontal rows, weaving your horizontal rows over and under the vertical rows. If you begin to run out of thread before you finish, complete a row and tape the thread on the inside of the card. Then, rethread your needle, tape the end of the thread to the inside, and begin a new row.

5 When you have finished all the rows, secure the thread on the inside of the card with tape, cut a square of accent or matching paper to cover the taped threads, and glue the square onto the inside cover. Put a piece of wax paper over the glued square, close the card, and weight it with a book while the glue dries.

VARIATIONS

As you experiment with variations on this basic design, you may decide to increase the size of your template slightly, position your rows of beads more closely together for a denser look, change the position of the grid on your card, or add other ornamentation.

Charmed Beaded Basket

DESIGN: **ALLISON STILWELL**

*After adding beaded wire and charms to
an existing wire base, it's hard to tell where
the original ends and your fancywork begins.
Contemporary home accessory stores carry wire
baskets of all kinds. They provide a perfect pattern
for attaching your own rows of ornamentation.*

1 Thread your needle with a 12-inch (31-cm)
piece of wire. Beginning at the base of your
basket, secure the wire by threading it around
a vertical piece of the basket frame, leaving a
1-inch (2.5-cm) tail, and twisting the tail around
the main piece of wire.

YOU WILL NEED

Purchased wire basket
(choose one with grid-like wiring)

Size 6 seed beads in a variety of colors
(Allison Stilwell used approximately three 30-gram
variety packs for the project shown)

Charms (you can purchase theme packs in craft stores
or use charms you've been saving for a project)

34-gauge silver wire (the project shown required
approximately one 24-yard [22-meter] spool)

Stiff needle

Wire cutters

VARIATION

This basic design would also work on a wicker
or rattan basket, which would likely be more
tightly woven than the basket shown here.
If so, the rows of beads would lie on top of the
basket frame, rather than in between the wider
rows of a wire basket.

2 Using the basket's horizontal pieces as a guide, you will be stringing beads in rows, traveling from vertical piece to vertical piece. To begin, string enough beads (in a random color pattern) onto your wire to travel from the place where you secured the wire to the basket's next vertical piece. You may need to push the beads gently over the twisted tail section. When you reach the second vertical piece, make a loop around it with your needle and wire to secure that section of beads, then continue on.

3 When you complete one row around the basket, wrap your wire up the vertical piece where you began the first row and start the next row above it. If you begin to run out of wire, twist your remaining wire around another piece of the basket to secure it and begin with a new strand. If your basket's vertical pieces are far apart and you want to secure your beads more firmly, each time you complete a row, you can go back over it, weaving your wire in between every few beads, securing the beaded wire section to the horizontal basket piece below it.

4 Create spokes of two strands of beaded wire each, moving from the center to the rim of the lid. After securing the end of each strand to the rim by wrapping the wire around a basket piece several times, weave back up over every few beads (as described in step 3) to hold the strand in place.

5 Add charms around the rim of the lid by threading each charm with wire, looping the wire through a piece of the lid frame (leaving a bit of wire so that the charm dangles), then wrapping the wire several times just above the charm to secure it. Snip the wire and press the clipped end against the wrapped section.

Fan Pull

DESIGN: **LYNN KRUCKE**

*Add some grace to the act of cooling off.
Whether this fan pull shimmers in the sunlight
on a veranda or dangles in your den,
its Victorian-era charm is irresistible.
Best of all, whipping one up
is a breeze.*

1 Cut three 10-inch (26-cm) lengths of jewelry twine and tie the lengths together near one end with a standard knot. Trim the twine above the knot to about ¼ inch (1 cm).

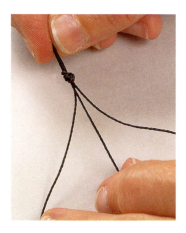

2 Thread all three lengths of twine through the hole in one end of a bead chain connector from the inside of the connector, going out through the hole. Pull the knot against the hole and dot the knot with glue.

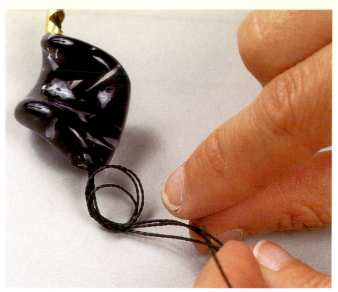

3 Thread all three lengths of twine through the large bead and tie a second knot snugly against the end of the bead. (If you have trouble threading the twine, treat the end of each length separately with a dot of glue to make it stiff.)

4 String beads on each length of twine separately in arrangements similar to the patterns shown. Each string of fringe will be a different length. Once you complete each strand, tie an overhand knot snugly against it and dot the knot with glue. Trim the twine once the glue is dry.

5 Attach the bead chain connector to a 5-inch (13-cm) length of bead chain, and attach the other end of the chain to a second connector.

VARIATIONS

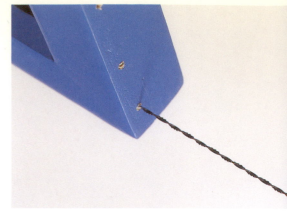

1 Drill holes 3/4 inch (2 cm) apart around the entire frame. Position the holes near the front edge of each side, avoiding the slot where the photo will be inserted.

Picture Frame

DESIGN: **TRACY PAGE STILWELL**

This project is a case study in how to make an ordinary object positively gleeful. A purchased picture frame goes from same-old-thing to spirited with some artfully arranged twists of wire and playful patterns of beads.

YOU WILL NEED

22-gauge wire

Several tablespoons of multicolored size 6 seed beads

Flat-sided wooden frame

Drill with $1/16$-inch (1.5-mm) drill bit

Wire cutters

Round-nose pliers

Chain-nose pliers

Glue

HOW TO

Making a Wire Spiral, page 17

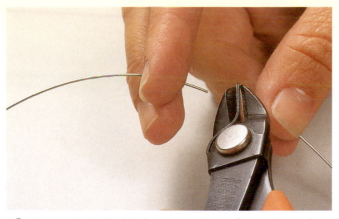

2 For each drilled hole, cut a piece of wire. Vary the lengths between 1¾ and 2½ inches (4.5 and 6.5 cm).

3 Create spirals at the end of each wire (see Making a Wire Spiral, page 17).

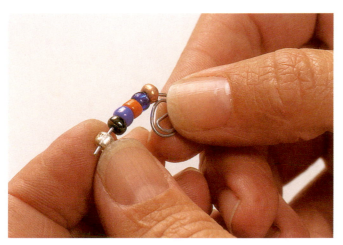

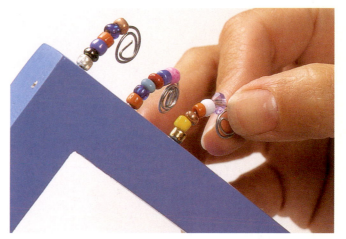

4 Add four to six beads in random color patterns to the straight end of the wire, leaving at least ¼ inch (1 cm) of wire on the straight end unbeaded.

5 Use an extra piece of wire as a tool to push a dot of glue into one of the drilled holes. Then, insert one of your decorated pieces of wire into the hole. Continue until one side is completed. To keep the wires in position until the glue sets, balance the frame at an angle (so the wires lean in the direction you want them to flow) as you work. Glue your beaded wires into the holes on all four sides of the frame, allowing each completed side to set for several minutes before you move on to the next one.

Bead-wrapped Bottle

DESIGN: MELANIE WOODSON

Purchase a decorative bottle from a craft or home-decorating shop (or recycle your own), match the glass with a few bold beads, and your gift-giving problems may be solved for good (you'll probably want to make a few for yourself too). Top your creation with a bottle pourer insert (available at kitchen stores), and it's a perfect vessel for everything from olive oil and vinegar to dish soap.

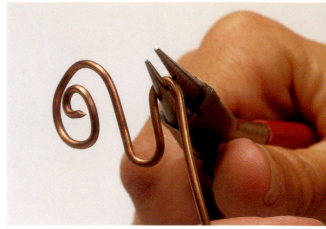

1 Using your pliers, coil one end of your copper wire. Bend it once in each direction above the coil, and pinch the corners with the pliers. These bends will create a "stopper" that holds the beads in place.

YOU WILL NEED

Bottle

Approximately 4 feet (1.5 meters)
of 8-gauge copper wire

Approximately one dozen large beads
of your choice, with holes large enough
to accommodate the wire

Round-nose pliers

VARIATIONS

Some of Melanie Woodson's other bead-wrapped bottles are featured on page 70.

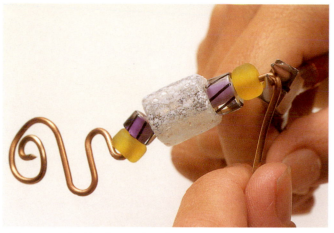

2 String half of your beads onto the wire. Bend the wire at a sharp angle above the arrangement to hold the beads in place at the top.

3 Hold the beaded coil against the bottle and wrap the wire around and up the bottle one and a half times. Don't worry about getting the wire tight at this point; you will be bending the wire later to take up any slack.

4 Bend the wire once in each direction again, pinch the corners, and string the rest of your beads. Bend the wire at a sharp angle above this second arrangement to hold the beads place. Twist the remaining wire up the bottle and around the neck several times. If you have a lot of extra wire, cut some off, making sure to leave enough to coil the top of the wire.

5 Hold the coil at the top against the front of the bottle with one hand. With your round-nose pliers, pinch the wire and give your pliers a quarter turn to the right. Continue this action all the way down the wire, always turning in the same direction, until the wire is tight and both sets of beads and both coils are on the front side of your bottle. It is important to get the wire on the neck of the bottle as tight as possible, but the wire on the body of the bottle will not lay completely flat.

Fringed Bookmark

DESIGN: **TERRY B. TAYLOR**

Use this design to create a rich, glittering device for saving your place. Fringed benefit: it's one more reason to have a good book going at all times.

1 Finger press or iron a ¼- to ½-inch (1- to 1.5-cm) fold at each end of the ribbon, enclosing the cut edge with a second fold to make a hem. If your ribbon does not hold the hem well, sew it in place.

YOU WILL NEED

Approximately 12 inches (31 cm) of ribbon (Try grosgrain, sheer organza, or any other ribbon material. Terry Taylor used a metallic ribbon.)

Several tablespoons of various small seed beads, including bugle beads, in complementary colors

5 accent beads

Beading thread or decorative sewing thread to match ribbon color

Beading needle

Scissors

Ruler

Iron

2 small, flat containers (such as jar lids)

HOW TO

Making Fringe, page 17

2 Pour small amounts (¼ teaspoon or less) of various colors of seed beads into one flat container and mix. Pour the larger accent beads into your second flat container. Thread your needle and knot the end. Starting at a bottom corner of one hem, anchor the knot inside the hem and take a small backstitch to prevent the knot from popping through the ribbon, especially if you are using a sheer or coarsely woven ribbon. (To backstitch, insert the needle behind your first stitch and come back up through the ribbon half a stitch ahead.)

3 Using your seed beads and your accent beads, create five pieces of dangled fringe across one end of your bookmark (see Making Fringe, page 17). End with your accent bead and a final seed bead. Your strands of fringe can vary in length.

4 To make the looped fringe, begin picking up seed beads with the needle in a random manner. String approximately 10 to 18 per loop, making the loops various sizes. Once a loop is complete, pass the needle back through the hem and make a tiny stitch to secure the hem. Continue to make loops across the entire hem. Create additional rows of beaded loops above the first row, staggering the loops in a shingle fashion.

5 When your loops are complete at one end, create loops on the other hemmed end in a similar fashion, though the ends need not be identical.

GALLERY OF BEADED OBJECTS

ABOVE: These classy key rings by **PHYLLIS EAGLE KALIONZES** were created by using head pins, jump rings, and standard wire loops and spirals. The wire-adorned beads of semi-precious stone attach to large split rings.

LEFT: These variations of the beaded bottle project on page 66 play with color, size, and various methods of stringing and twisting wire.

MELANIE WOODSON

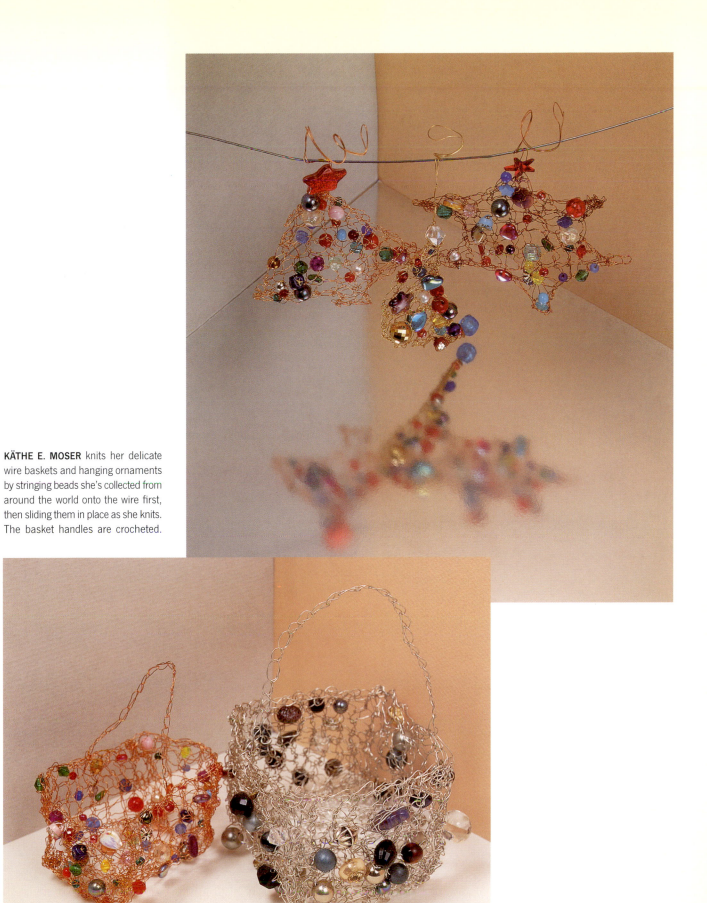

KÄTHE E. MOSER knits her delicate wire baskets and hanging ornaments by stringing beads she's collected from around the world onto the wire first, then sliding them in place as she knits. The basket handles are crocheted.

LEFT: From simple stringing patterns to advanced bead-weaving stitches, these containers and jars span the beading spectrum. The tin container and tiny cardboard box incorporate basic designs, while the woven jars use a peyote stitch, a popular bead-weaving stitch.

MELANIE WOODSON

BELOW LEFT: Want to guarantee a flashy finished product? Begin with a beading base that has flair, like this unusual golden mesh bag, purchased at a home accessory store. Metallic thread, masks, and beads of bone and stone create a jungle-motif container that could be used for everything from storing lotions and potions to delivering a bottle of wine.

TRACY PAGE STILWELL

BELOW: This frame was treated with a two-tone finish, then embellished with ink stamps. The ceramic letter beads were strung through drilled holes with satin cord. Don't limit the design (ideal for personalizing frames for children) to names only—how about the date of an event, or "Happy Birthday," "School Days," or other captions?

LYNN KRUCKE

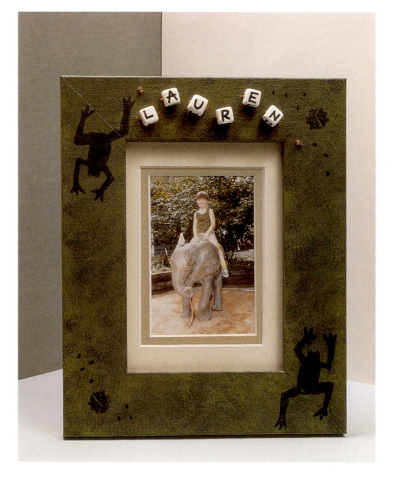

LEFT: Lamp shade frames wrapped with beaded wire are all the rage for making dark corners glitter. The quality of light you can create is endless. Translucent beads let lots of light through, while more opaque beads provide a diffused, romantic glow.

JUDY HELLER

BELOW LEFT: Designer **TRACY PAGE STILWELL** transformed a manufactured muslin doll into a "Garden Spirit," complete with vining seed beads, garden tool charms, and a hook in the back for hanging in a potting shed (where she's sure to bring good luck and promote healthy growth). The playful concept lends itself to talismans of all kinds, from kitchen fairies to nymphs and pixies to watch over your work space.

BELOW: These dainty flowers are simply strands of artfully twisted wire adorned with tiny seed beads.

JUDY HELLER

RIGHT: This circular design of loops and fringe creates a draping collar, suitable for everything from fishbowls to centerpieces.

LYNN KRUCKE

BELOW: You may decide you enjoy beads most when you're using them in unexpected ways—turning drab, everyday objects like this flowerpot into original works of art.

MELANIE WOODSON

BELOW RIGHT: These kaleidoscopes are an imaginative example of how fade-into-the-background knick-knacks can take on showpiece status once they're adorned with beads.

SUSAN KINNEY

Beaded fringe and dangles come to life when illuminated by candlelight. Metal frames can be strung with fringe, heavy glass can be wrapped with wire. Entire table settings can be studded with beads that glitter and glow.

Votive Candle Holder
ALLISON STILWELL

Candles and Goblet
SUSAN KINNEY

The 38 strands of cobalt glass that create this stunning, 27-inch by 28½-inch (69-cm by 72-cm) light catcher are strung on tigertail and hang from a piece of oak.

ONE TRIBAL VILLAGE

CONTRIBUTING DESIGNERS

KIMBERLEY ADAMS is a lampwork bead artist who also designs jewelry for the distinctive beads she creates. Together with her husband Paul, she manages her growing bead business. She is a featured artist in many galleries and shops, and teaches lampwork on a regular basis. Special acknowledgment also goes to Kimberley's in-house artists, Ian, 9, and Jordan, 7, who used her design to create the napkin rings featured on page 52.

MELANIE ALTER is a founder of the New Mexico Bead Society and a jewelry designer who utilizes beads, charms, and findings from around the world. In addition, she started Melanie Collection, which markets beads and ornamentation through a mail-order catalog.

HELEN BANES is a fiber artist and jewelry designer with a background in painting, fiber, and metal techniques. She is a founding member of the Fiberworks Gallery in Alexandria, Virginia, and former president of The Bead Society of Greater Washington. Her jewelry has been showcased at national and international exhibits, including the Smithsonian exhibit: Good as Gold, Alternative Materials in American Jewelry.

JUDY HELLER was a controller for many years, teaching beading when her schedule allowed. Now, she is the class coordinator for Beadworks in Boston, and she focuses on beading and teaching full time.

TRACY HILDEBRAND designs jewelry that incorporates glass beads she makes using lampworking techniques. She also teaches glass bead making classes in Asheville, North Carolina, and sells her handmade beads. For ordering information, call 828-259-9319.

PHYLLIS EAGLE KALIONZES, a founding member of Ten Women, an artists' co-op gallery in Santa Monica, California, uses vintage beads from the 1920s, 30s, and 40s from Czechoslovakia, Italy, and Bohemia in much of her work. She also makes her own glass beads and incorporates other interesting objects into her work. In one series of earrings, she used pieces of her mother's wedding crystal, shattered in a California earthquake in 1994.

SUSAN KINNEY is a designer specializing in eclectic interiors, glass and clay jewelry, fabric and rug design, and computer-generated artwork. She attributes the Oriental influence in many of her designs to her years living in Japan and Hawaii. She can be reached at her interior design business, Suezen Designs, in Asheville, North Carolina, at designdr@mindspring.com.

LYNN KRUCKE lives in Summerville, South Carolina, with her husband and daughter. She has long been fascinated with handcrafts of all types, and her favorite projects incorporate elements from more than one craft. She particularly enjoys beading, and beads are likely to pop up in almost any project.

NANCY MCGAHA feels that living in the mountains of western North Carolina has enhanced her creative spirit. She enjoys working in a variety of media, including beading, smocking, weaving, creating fiber arts, and any combination of these.

KÄTHE E. MOSER learned to knit from her grandmother when she was six years old, and considers it a joy and a therapy. In addition to knitting beaded wire objects, which she sells throughout the Asheville, North Carolina, area, she knits sweaters and jackets and is experimenting with dyeing her own yarn.

LINDA ROSE NALL has been working with wire since 1989. She now focuses primarily on stained-glass functional items and jewelry.

ONE TRIBAL VILLAGE is the collaborative design venture of Adam and Y'mani of Asheville, North Carolina. They use beads to combine color, texture, size, style, and shape with simplicity, striving to evoke a sense of unity and diversity that is the common theme in all of their designs. Many of their beads are handmade by artisans from around the world.

JEAN WALL PENLAND is an artist who paints and teaches in the mountains of western North Carolina. She has received both Pollack-Krasner and Adolph and Esther Gottlieb Foundation grants in support of her work.

ALLISON STILWELL is a Rhode Island artist who began by working with textiles and making quilts and dolls. She now enjoys working with almost all media, creating a wide range of projects.

TRACY PAGE STILWELL creates dolls, quilts, painted furniture, and mixed media projects. She is also known as a teacher, student, and curator, and can often be found in the garden.

KERRI SULLIVAN is a college student in Asheville, North Carolina, and has lived and traveled extensively overseas. She developed her addiction to beads when she landed a job at a bead store.

TERRY B. TAYLOR wishes he could make a living producing and selling the many items he creates. As the next best thing, he is the catalog coordinator for Lark Books Catalog.

CAROLE TRIPP, who trained in clothing and textile design, owns and operates Creative Castle, a bead supply store in Newbury Park, California. She designs beadwork, teaches beading classes, and designs and manufactures jewelry kits.

MELANIE WOODSON is a multi-talented craftsperson who lives and works in Asheville, North Carolina. Beading is just one of her loves; she also works in media such as metal, mosaics, glass, and polymer clay.

BARBARA WRIGHT strings beads almost as often as she breathes. She has taught hundreds of people the ins and outs of basic jewelry making.

ACKNOWLEDGMENTS

Thanks to the people and businesses who
provided expertise and encouragement
along the way— and all we needed,
from beads to background details,
to create the photos in this book.

Barry Olen, Barbara Wright,
and others at Beads and Beyond
in Asheville, North Carolina
(Thanks not only for the
boxes of props, but for the
countless hours of advice!)

Deborah Coule at Chevron
Trading Post & Bead Co.,
Asheville, North Carolina

The Natural Home,
Asheville, North Carolina

Danielle Truscott Dawson,
for lending her locks for the
hair sticks on pages 44 and 48

Tracy Hildebrand,
an indispensable advisor,
whose expert hands lead you through
the how-to steps
for each project!

For more information about
Lark Books visit our website at
www.larkbooks.com

INDEX

Adhesive, industrial-strength, 12

Anvil and jewelry hammer, 16

Bead caps, 14

Bead cement, 12

Bead glue, 12

Bead shapes, 9

Bead sizes, 9

Bead thread, 10

Bead tips, 13, clamshell, 13

Beading wire, 10

Bugle beads, 10

Cement, bead, 12

Clasps, 12

Color, using in design, 18

Cord, 11

Crimp beads, 13

Delicas, 9

Earring findings, 14

Elastic cord, 11

Eye pins, 14

Findings, 13

Fringe, making, 17

Head pins, 14

Hemp cord, 11

Jump rings, 14, opening, 14

Leather cord, 11

Needles, 11

Pliers, 15

Rattail, 11

Seed beads, 9

Size and shape in design, 19

Spacers, 14

Stringing patterns, 22

Texture and character in design, 20

Thread, 10

Tigertail, 10

Waxed linen cord, 11

Wire, 11, memory, 11

Wire cutters, 15

Wire loop, making, 16

Wire file, 16

Wire spiral, making, 17

A NOTE ABOUT SUPPLIERS

Usually, the supplies you need for making the projects in Lark books can be found at your local craft supply store, discount mart, home improvement center, or retail shop relevant to the topic of the book. Occasionally, however, you may need to buy materials or tools from specialty suppliers. In order to provide you with the most up-to-date information, we have created a listing of suppliers on our Website, which we update on a regular basis. Visit us at www.larkbooks.com, click on "Craft Supply Sources," and then click on the relevant topic. You will find numerous companies listed with their web address and/or mailing address and phone number.